Families

Grandparents

Rebecca Rissman

Heinemann Library
Chicago, Illinois

www.heinemannraintree.com

Visit our website to find out more information about Heinemann-Raintree books.

To order:

☎ Phone 888-454-2279

💻 Visit www.heinemannraintree.com
to browse our catalog and order online.

Edited by Rebecca Rissman and Catherine Veitch
Designed by Ryan Frieson
Picture research by Tracy Cummins
Originated by Capstone Global Library Ltd
Printed and bound in China by Leo Paper Products Ltd

14 13 12 11 10
10 9 8 7 6 5 4 3 2 1

Library of Congress Cataloging-in-Publication Data
Rissman, Rebecca.
  Grandparents / Rebecca Rissman.
    p. cm.—(Families)
  Includes bibliographical references and index.
  ISBN 978-1-4329-4658-6 (hc)—ISBN 978-1-4329-4666-1
(pb) 1. Grandparents—Juvenile literature. 2. Families—Juvenile
literature. I. Title.
  HQ759.9.R57 2011
  306.874'5—dc22   2010016994

Acknowledgments
We would like to thank the following for permission to reproduce photographs: Corbis pp.**10** (©Markus Moellenberg), **14** (©Kevin Dodge), **19** (©Nils Hendrik Muller/Cultura), **20** (©Kristy-Anne Glubish/Design Pics), **23 c** (©Markus Moellenberg); Getty Images pp. **4** (Sylvain Grandadam), **7** (Stephen Chiang), **8** (Tony Metaxas), **9** (Jupiterimages), **11** (Jay Reilly), **13** (Manoj Adlukay), **16** (Ron Levine), **17** (Image Source), **18** (Alex Mares-Manton), **21** (Ariel Skelley), **23 a** (Manoj Adlukay); istockphoto pp. **5** (©Ann Marie Kurtz), **22** (©Diane Labombarbe); Photolibrary pp. **12** and **23 b** (both Radius Images); Shutterstock pp. **6** (©Mehmet Dilsiz), **15** (©Yarek Gora).

Front cover photograph of a granddaughter kissing her grandmother reproduced with permission of Getty Images (China Tourism Press). Back cover photograph of a granddaughter helping her grandfather with his tie reproduced with permission of Corbis (©Nils Hendrik Muller/Cultura).

We would like to thank Anne Pezalla and Nancy Harris for their invaluable help in the preparation of this book.

Every effort has been made to contact copyright holders of any material reproduced in this book. Any omissions will be rectified in subsequent printings if notice is given to the publisher.

Contents

What Is a Family?

A family is a group of people who care for each other.

People in a family are different ages.

All families are different.

All families are special.

What Are Families Like?

Some families like to play games.

Some families like to cook together.

Who Are Grandparents?

Some families have parents. Parents are adults who have children.

grandparent

Parents have parents, too!

They are called grandparents.

Different Grandparents

Your parent's mother is
your grandmother.

Your parent's father is
your grandfather.

Some families have
many grandparents.

Some families have few grandparents.
Some families do not have any
grandparents.

Some grandparents live far from their families.

Some grandparents live with
their families.

Some grandparents care for their grandchildren.

Some grandchildren help care for their grandparents.

Some families visit their grandparents at special homes.

Do you have grandparents?

Family Tree

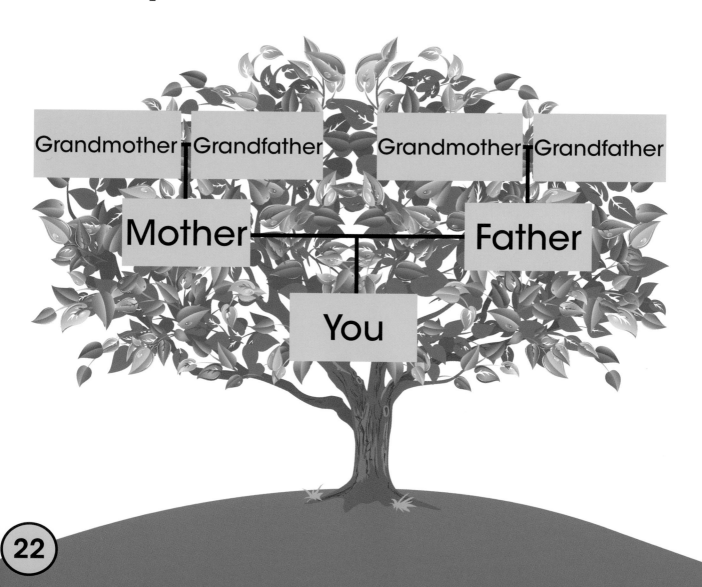

Grandmother Grandfather Grandmother Grandfather

Mother Father

You

Picture Glossary

grandfather your parent's father

grandmother your parent's mother

parent adult who has children

Index

Note to Parents and Teachers
Before Reading
Explain to children that people in families are often related to each other. Most children are related to their parents. And parents have parents, too! They are a child's grandparents!

After Reading
Ask children if they have special nicknames for their grandparents, such as Grammy or Papa. Make a list of these names on the board.